Search Engine

Optimisation, the Basics

Jargon-free. Best Practice.

By Heather Robinson

Contents

About the Author

Heather Robinson has been helping businesses and organisations get the most out of the internet since 2005. Helping them to define and implement effective marketing strategies, manage budgets, and deliver the best results possible in line with achieving their goals.

As a marketing graduate, Heather has worked in all areas of marketing, but her passion lies with digital technologies, utilising platforms such as Google AdWords, social media networks and email marketing to maximise exposure for her clients and driving a constant flow of traffic to their website.

In 2012, Heather set up 'Skittish', a boutique digital agency in the north of England with the aim of helping small to medium sized businesses get a good grasp of all the opportunities available to them in the online world. Her clients vary from 'one-man-band' and micro businesses to larger, multinational companies.

A lot of Heather's time is dedicated to delivering training and talks in her area of expertise, running regular workshops aimed at business owners on areas such as search engine marketing strategy and creating a content marketing plan. She also speaks regularly at local, national and global digital marketing conferences and has written and contributed to several books aimed at helping the small business owner.

Other publications include:
Essential Online Advertising (2014)
Email Marketing Success (2015)
Available from oodlebooks.com

Easy Business Blogging from Scratch (2015)
Available on Amazon.com

Introduction

Search Engine Optimisation (or SEO as it's often abbreviated to) is seen as a bit of a mystery and often dubbed a 'dark art'. Simply put, SEO is just the process of improving a website's visibility in search results so that when someone searches for your products or services, your website will be found quickly and hopefully at the top of the first page where your potential customers are likely to click to visit your site. When your site is at the top of Google's search results it has the potential to generate income for your business 24/7.

With the launch of Google in 1998, we saw the first major search engine quickly grow to popularity and dominate the search market. It was not only used as a search engine, but also a default home page for many internet users meaning more and more journeys online began with Google.

In 2006, the verb 'to google' was added to the Oxford English Dictionary meaning to search. Although there are many search engines out there such as Bing, Google remains the frontrunner in the UK with around 90% market share (source: http://bit.ly/uksearchmarket). This can often mean that when we talk about search engine optimisation, we're often really referring to Google optimisation and the terms search engine and Google can be interchangeable.

If you're reading this from outside the UK, you'll see a different picture, with more Bing users in the United States, for example, Google only holds around a 67% market share (source: http://bit.ly/ussearchmarket). And in countries like China where Google doesn't dominate, they only have around 10% of the search market with over 80% of internet users favouring Baidu (source: http://bit.ly/chinasearchmarket).

Since the launch of search engines, businesses have seen the benefit of being positioned on the first page of search results. By being number one in search results, you will be appearing above your competition and should see the highest amount of traffic coming to your website from these results. This additional traffic leads to more brand awareness and, ultimately, more sales.

It's because of these benefits that the practice of optimising websites (and making a living from doing it) became common place and SEO agencies are now in abundance.

Using an SEO agency or consultant is often a good idea if you are short on time and expertise in this area, but even with someone else managing your SEO campaigns, it's always a good idea to know the basics yourself.

Sadly, the SEO industry does get some negative press with many people paying for SEO work that doesn't deliver results or, even worse, delivers a penalty. I believe many problems stem from a lack of communication between the agency and the client and issues with managing expectations. SEO isn't a one-off process that will deliver results immediately; it's a long term investment that requires hard work and a lot of time.

This reputation for being something secretive and underhand has done the SEO industry no favours.

I've been involved in SEO since 2005 and have seen and witnessed the strangest tactics to get websites ranking on the first page of Google, some good but a lot that are very bad. I've worked with other SEO professionals and agencies and seen firsthand how client relationships break down which leaves the client disillusioned, confused and often out of pocket.

It's important to note that there are no guarantees with SEO. We cannot control what Google does so any company who guarantees you results should be avoided (or interrogated as to how they can guarantee results!). It's also common for SEO campaigns to take time to have any major effect and you could be waiting several months to see your website move up the ranks, so be prepared to invest long term.

By reading this book, you should have a better understanding of how search engines work and what is involved in optimising a website. Many of the tips given in this books should be actionable by you if you have access to your website to make changes. Even if you choose to outsource SEO, you will have the tools to be able to communicate more effectively with your agency and know whether you are getting value for money and the results you should expect.

1. How do search engines work?

Search engines like Google are designed to provide a user with relevant results based on a search query they enter into the search box. Search engines, therefore, have two jobs. The first is to find all the information on the internet and store it logically and the second is to be able to locate that information and order it by relevance when someone searches for it.

For search engines to be able to find the information on the internet, they need to send out what's known as spiders or bots that 'crawl' the internet, following links between pages and websites to discover new content. Links between pages and websites are what makes the internet a 'world wide web'. Without links, the internet would be a very lonely place and not half as useful as it is today!

One of the things I hear a lot is from business owners who have just had a website built and they often complain that their website isn't working or they can't find it when they search for it. This is usually due to the fact that there are no other websites linking to it, therefore Google has yet to find it.

Without any links to your site, it exists almost like an island with no means of communication with the rest of the world wide web. Once other websites start to include links to your site, Google will find it. This can be as simple as adding a listing on Yell.com or other relevant business directories.

Search engines then need to store the information they find online and they do this in data centres across the globe. These are huge storage facilities housing servers that contain information. If you're into your IT and want to learn more about Google's data centres, visit: www.google.co.uk/about/datacenters/.

The next job of the search engine is then to reorganise this information into some kind of system so that the information can be easily found and delivered in a logical order to someone searching for it. To do this, search engines use computer programs known as algorithms. When we talk about Google updates and changes in the search results, these are down to changes in Google's algorithm. The algorithm is responsible for displaying your website in the position in which it appears when someone searches for your products and services and, as such, has a lot to answer for!

According to Google's website "Google's mission is to organise the world's information and make it universally accessible and useful."

For Google and other search engines to be successful, they have to provide the most relevant and useful results to searchers in order to keep them coming back. Google is also a business at the end of the day and it makes the majority of its income from the paid advertisements in the search results. The more people who use Google to search for things across the internet, the more people will click on the paid listings and the more money Google will make.

What this means for you and your website is that you have to make it clear to search engines what your website, and each page within it, is about. The more information you can give the search engines, the more likely it is that your website will be deemed relevant for a user's search query.

It's all common sense stuff when you break it down, but so often overlooked when websites are built. In the next chapter we'll look at how you can optimise your website and let the search engines know exactly what your website is all about.

2.   How do I make my website search engine friendly?

SEO is often split into two forms: 'on-page' and 'off-page'. On-page SEO is the process of making adjustments to your website content and code behind the website in order to improve its relevancy to your keywords (words or phrases you want to see your website rank in search results for).

Off-page SEO is the process of improving your presence elsewhere on the internet through third party websites. We'll cover this in Chapter 4.

The focus of this chapter will be making a website easy to crawl by search engine bots and how to carry out on-page optimisation.

You may have heard the term 'search engine friendly' before, but what does it actually mean? If your site is search engine friendly, it basically means that the code behind the site is easily crawled and indexed by search engines.

The term is often confused with being search engine optimised and I have heard on a number of occasions about people who are sold a website built on WordPress, for example, and have been told that it will naturally rank well in Google because WordPress is 'search engine friendly'.

Whilst I agree that WordPress is a superb platform to build your website and it can indeed be search engine friendly, it doesn't, however, come optimised straight out of the box. You do need to make adjustments to truly optimise your website and this goes beyond installing an SEO plugin; you actually have to understand how SEO works and be able to manually optimise each page and post on your WordPress site to get the full benefits.

Google's algorithm looks at over two hundred factors when it ranks each page on your website and no one will ever be sure what all those factors are, but there are several major factors that we can be pretty sure you need to be aware of and it's these that we will cover here.

Page Title
The Page Title is what Google displays as the blue clickable link in the search results.

It's also used across the web browser's tab and will appear when you hover over it with your mouse. Plus it's saved as the default name for the page in your favourites or bookmarks.

It doesn't appear anywhere else on your page, but will (or should) be present in your website's code. To identify the page title in your code, simply browse to your website and right click somewhere on the page and select 'View source' or 'View page source' depending on which browser you use.

To find the page title, press Ctrl + F then search for "<title>" (without the quotation marks). You should find something that looks like this:

```
<title>Skittish Digital Marketing Consultancy
- SEO, AdWords, Social Media</title>
```

Google loves to see an optimised page title. It reads this to decide what each page on your website is about and decides whether it is relevant to the searcher's query. For page titles to be optimised they should:

- include keywords and phrases you expect your site to be ranked for
- Keep it below 60 characters including spaces - 50 - 55 is the optimum to avoid Google cutting it short with '...' as we saw in the example above
- place the most important keywords at the beginning - it lets Google know that you consider these words to be important so it should treat them the same
- include your company or brand name - this can improve click through rate and brand awareness

The worst mistake I see a lot is having 'Home' as the title of the home page and 'About' as the title of the about page. It may sound logical to do this, but what does this tell Google about what the page or the website is about? You have 50 - 60 characters, so use them wisely!

Meta Description

The meta description is used by Google to display a few lines of text beneath your listing in the search results.

Although the meta description is said not to influence the search results, it can influence whether or not searchers click on your listing over the competition's.

Google will highlight keywords within the meta description by making them bold, helping the searcher to see the relevancy of the listing to what they are searching for.

You should see the meta description in the code close to the <title> tag and it should be something you can change if you have access to edit your website.

Headings

The headings on your page are key for Google to understand what the page is about and how the information is structured. With this information, Google can determine how relevant your website is for the person searching for your products or services.

Within the code of your website, headings will be marked up using HTML tags like these:

```
<h1>Main Heading</h1>
<h2>Sub Heading</h2>
<h3>Lesser Sub Heading</h3>
<h4>...etc, etc
```

Heading tags are numbered from 1 down as far as 6 in some cases, where 1 is the main heading for the page and headings with higher numbers are subheadings.

I often see websites that don't use this markup and are therefore missing a <h1> tag. It's vital to include a <h1> and advisable to have <h2> tags as well.

To check if your website uses heading tags, simply browse to your website and right click anywhere on the screen and select 'View Source' or 'View Page Source'. Then search for a <h1> tag using Ctrl+F on your keyboard.

Your headings should be relevant to the content on the page and include keywords where possible. As an example, if you are a business coach, you may have a page on your website which gives information about coaching plans for start up businesses. Your headings, therefore, may look something like this:

```
<h1>Startup Business Coaching</h1>
<p>...Introductory text about the
service...</p>
<h2>Monthly Coaching Plans for
Startup Businesses</h2>
<p>...Details about the monthly
plans...</p>
<h2>Startup Business Strategy
Meeting</h2>
<p>...Details about one-off strategy
meetings...</p>
<h3>Startup Business Coaching
Pricing</h3>
<p>...Details of costs associated with your
service...</p>
```

Using headings and subheadings within your
website text will also help to break up the
information, making it easier to read for human
visitors too, so it's definitely a win-win.

Content
Probably the most important part of your
website is the text you use. Sadly, it's often
overlooked in favour of large images, videos and
that minimalist look as people argue that 'no one
reads websites'.

I agree to some extent that it's rare to see people sit and read an entire website like they would a book, however, Google loves to read websites. If we don't give Google anything to read, we risk leaving it in the dark about our website and what we do.

Large photos, graphics and video do look stunning on modern websites and it's often what the visitor likes to see, however, there must be a balance in order to keep Google happy too.

Google cannot see images, it cannot watch videos and it doesn't really care how fancy your website looks. Google loves content full stop.

Aim to have around three paragraphs of text on each page of your website, or roughly 300 words. It may sound like a lot, but it will set you apart from other image heavy sites.

Your text should be written for humans first and foremost. Whilst I'm going to advise you to use keywords in your text, I don't mean to artificially stuff keywords into every sentence for the sake of Google.

The important thing to remember is to optimise each page of your website for one keyword or phrase and any slight variations.

Don't try to optimise a page for every product or service you provide.

This can get tricky when you're looking at your home page as you often want to let everyone know about everything you do on this page.

My advice is to focus your attention on optimising internal pages (those that are one or two clicks away from your home page like product pages, service pages, about page, etc) for the keyword or phrase that people will search for.

Your home page will naturally rank well as it's often the page people will link to and it's the page that Google will crawl most often. Think about optimising this page for your company or brand name or a keyword that sums up everything you do.

Going back to the above example of a business coach, your internal pages could be optimised for phrases such as 'startup business coaching', 'business planning', 'business strategy', whereas your homepage could be optimised for simply 'business coaching', or 'ABC Business Associates'.

A note on keyword density

Many SEO articles and sources will talk about 'keyword density' - i.e. the number of times you use your keyword on a page divided by the number of total words. It's important to remember that that any rules regarding keyword density are usually invented by people outside of Google, and there's no official guideline from Google regarding the number of times you should use a keyword on a page.

Therefore, don't worry too much about the keyword density of your text. Focus instead on creating valuable content that appeals to the user. Explain how you help your clients, what problems they may have and how you solve them.

How do your services or your approach to delivering them differ to the competition? Use your content to make you stand out from the many other people doing what you do. And don't forget a strong call to action - what do you want your website visitors to do after they have read your content? Pick up the phone and call you? Submit an enquiry form? Download a document? Enter a competition?

Focusing your content on your users will create a website that converts visitors into customers. Focusing your content on search engines may create a high ranking website, but nothing more.

Images

Images play a vital role in your website for users. They help to illustrate your point, break up long passages of text and give the user an instant understanding of what your website is about (assuming your images are relevant!). But as I've mentioned before, Google cannot see the images, no matter how good they are. What Google sees is the HTML code used to place an image in a web page.

This code should look something like this:

```
<img
src="http://example.com/path/to/image
file.jpg" alt="Beautiful image of…"
width="300" height="250" />
```

Google will read the 'alt' attribute to determine what the picture is of. It is therefore important to make sure you add a description of the image between the speech marks. It's also a good idea to include keywords in this if that is appropriate.

If you update your own website, you should be given the option to add an alt attribute (or alternate text) when you upload a new image.

Google may also look at the image file name, so it's worth renaming image files with a description of the image rather than the standard DCS004567.jpg (or similar!) that your digital camera may decide is an appropriate filename.

The alt attribute is also read aloud by screen reading software for visually impaired users. Having a descriptive alt attribute is therefore great for making your website more accessible.

If you don't have an alt attribute, the screen reader will read aloud the filename of the image – another reason to change the names of your image files!

Coding

It's something we don't see as an internet user, but the HTML and CSS code behind every website is what makes it function. It tells the browser how to display your content and what content to display.

Whilst the code may not mean much to you, it's the code that Google reads when it visits your website. It's the same code you can see when you right click your mouse and 'view source'.

This is the source code for your website.

Google likes to see clean code with no unnecessary code that will take time to read and even slow down the loading speed of your website.

This is where you may need to contact your web developer or at least get the advice of one.

Basically, you want to make sure your website does not contain nested tables (tables were once the standard way to lay out website content, but this is now outdated and adds a lot of unnecessary code), or frames (again this used to be a way of laying out web pages where different sections of a website like the header, menu and footer were contained in separate HTML documents).

You also need to consider the use of technology such as Flash. This can slow down the loading speed of your site and isn't accessible to Google. It's also not supported on many mobile devices, so any Flash elements of your website should have a substitute for mobile and tablet viewers.

Navigation
The key to great website usability is the ease of navigating from one page to another and finding the information you need quickly. Google will navigate your website in a similar way to users in that it follows links on your page.

Ideally you want your website links to be text rather than images. If you have buttons that link to another page, the text on those buttons should not be embedded in the button image, it should be text over a background image.

To see whether your text is embedded in buttons, you can click and drag your mouse over the button. If the text highlights on its own, it's text over an image. If the whole image highlights, chances are the text is embedded which isn't what you want.

For the best user experience, ensure all the information on your website is accessible within 1 or 2 clicks from the home page. Don't make people search and search, sending them down a rabbit warren to find the information they need.

By making the content on your site easy to find, you'll also be helping Google out too as it will be able to find, crawl and index all the content on your website quickly and easily.

Google wants to provide the best user experience for searchers looking for information, so if your website offers a great user experience, Google will look on your website more favourably, so always put the user first and Google will follow!

This chapter has covered some of the technical issues around website design which can affect your Google rankings and it may be that you need some expert help to implement some of these changes.

In Chapter 6 I'll show you some useful tools that you can use to start optimising your website. All you need is access to the source code of your site (or a friendly web developer who is happy to help!).

3. Will social media help with search engine positions?

If you want to know what is popular and relevant right now then you have to use social media to find out, it's where the world gossips.

What's being talked about, good or bad, is going to be on Facebook and Twitter.

It's also where people discover new products and brands every day and is a great opportunity for you to get your brand in front of a new audience.

In this chapter, I'm assuming you already have a social media strategy and are building it into your marketing activities, using it to react to what is being talked about in your niche in real time.

One belief many people have that stops them having a social strategy is that social networking has no benefit for their search engine optimisation strategy.

They would rather focus on organic search engine traffic. And if you ask 10 experts whether social media impacts SEO, you will get 10 different expert answers.

So, does social media impact on your SEO, and if so how can you develop a strategy for it to do just that?

What Elements Of Social Networking Could Affect SEO?

When it comes to the expert opinions, they are completely divided on the impact social signals can have on your Google rankings.

Some will point to industry reports, such as SearchMetrics SEO Ranking Factors Report, and show you that seven of the top 10 ranking factors in that report included social signals.

But then other experts point to Moz's Search Engine Ranking Factors Report where the data suggests that correlation does not equal causation.

I'm going to nail my flag to the mast and state that the truth is somewhere in between.

Direct social signals, such as volumes of tweets, retweets and Facebook likes are never going to be part of the future. They are too easily gamed.

But where I think social signals can directly affect rankings is through establishing and building trust. This links in to trying to establish a brand for yourself.

Branding creates trust with Google and by demonstrating quality through social media accounts that link to your branded websites, I think in the future, if not now, high quality social media accounts can affect the trust, and therefore the ranking, of the main site.

How Else Can Social Media Potentially Benefit SEO?

There are several indirect ways that social media can positively affect the rankings of your site.

You may not have considered how these can work, so I will run through the main ways here.

1. Link building potential

Quality activity on social media helps to increase awareness around your brand. Awareness leads to familiarity, which leads to trust.

Once people trust you they are more likely to share your content. Some of these people will be inspired by your content to create their own, and if they are honest they will link to you within it when they reference a point you have made.

Quality engagement on social media can also lead to people contacting you to guest blog for them, or for an opinion from an article they are writing, both of which can build links.

2. Search personalisation

Google+ users are given more personalised search results when they are logged in to their account. If you are using social media to link with that person then the result is that you are possibly going to rank more highly in their search results because of that connection.

3. Improved visitor metrics

High quality engagement on social media can increase visitors to your website. When people visit your site via Google it can result in a higher ranking because Google recognises that more people are looking for your site, which Google trusts.

You will also build trust with Google, and therefore improve your search engine rankings, if you demonstrate that people are staying on your website and engaging with it.

By building traffic through social media you are sending interested people to your website. This can lower your bounce rate, increase page views and time spent on your website. The better these metrics are, the more your site could benefit in organic (unpaid/natural) search results.

On a side note, if your site is a fast loading, responsive design then you will also benefit from a small rankings boost due to good site load times and being mobile friendly.

How Can I Use Social Media To Improve My SEO?

Like link building, a social media strategy with the goal of improving your search results can never really be called "optimisation".

What you are actually doing is trying to build signals to your website that Google will see as positive votes for the quality and relevance of your site, with the reward being a higher ranking.

So when it comes to social media, how can you develop a strategy that targets SEO improvement?

Well, we've already covered how briefly above. High quality engagement on social media will build trust, which will lead to natural link building, better quality traffic and sharing of your content.

There are ways you can help to improve your chances of this, through targeting who you follow. Let's look at a quick example now.

Targeting Social Media Users Who Can Improve Your SEO

Let's say your niche is health and fitness. You want to improve your engagement on social media with people who are likely to undertake actions that can boost your SEO.

This means you are looking for people who are active on social media and highly interested in health and fitness.

Your strategy could go as follows:

1. Find a large and highly targeted Twitter account in the health and fitness niche.
2. Create an account on Followerwonk.com (part of Moz.com).
3. Use Followerwonk to get detailed data on all the followers of the account you targeted.

4. Download the data as a spreadsheet. From there you can look at things such as how often people retweet tweets from the target account, what their following count is, and what their follower count is.

5. Filter the spreadsheet to only display Twitter users who retweet the target account frequently and who have good following rates.

This will give you a list of people who are actively engaged in the exact niche you want to target, who are happy to retweet accounts they follow, and are likely to follow you.

Use your own Twitter account to add high quality content to your tweets and then follow the people you targeted.

Now this method is obviously only one of many, and is not perfect. But it will allow you to target people who are more likely to engage with you and demonstrate behaviours to Google that can improve your search engine rankings. It will also help you to focus on creating quality content to share and provide value to your website visitors - things that Google loves!

Social Media Should Be an Integral Part of Your SEO Strategy

Social media activity can influence your rankings in the same way that link building can, and in many ways influence them in a superior way to pure link building.

This chapter is not everything you will need to develop a complete social media strategy, but hopefully it has shown you how important it is for more than engagement.

As a final thought, you always have to look to the future and try and predict it when it comes to Google.

Social media isn't going away. It is only going to get bigger. This means that even if Google is unsure how they are going to do it now, in the future social signals will affect rankings more and more.

4. What else can I do to get my website found in Google?

Make your site mobile friendly
On 21st April 2015, Google released its first specifically mobile algorithm update making the mobile-friendliness of your website a ranking factor.

When a Google update can trash your entire online presence overnight, there is no real surprise that rumours around Google's update relating to mobile friendly websites caused genuine unrest.

As with everything relating to Google updates it's vital that you cut through the rubbish to clearly understand what you need to do, or not do.

In this section I'm going to tell you everything you need to know about Google's mobile friendly update so that you can begin the process of putting your mind at rest and reacting right now.

What were the changes Google made to its algorithm?

Desktop is dying and is being replaced in the home by tablets and smartphones. The future of the Internet lies in mobile and it's this consumer shift which Google was looking to address.

The background to this update is that in 2014 search results started appearing with the term "Mobile friendly" next to them. A few industry people also spotted that some search results were also being labelled with the word "Slow".

It appears this was the beginning of the process that led up to the mobile-friendly update. Websites were starting to be analysed as either being mobile friendly, or not. Once the benchmarks had been clarified, Google felt confident in rolling out guidelines ready for a full update.

The search giant also rolled out changes to its apps, the Google Play platform and guidelines for developers in relation to mobile. On top of that, the presentation of some SERPs (Search Engine Results Pages) has also changed, especially on mobile devices, as Google pulls in real-world data.

My best guess is that Google will launch a completely new mobile web crawler, probably with an Android user agent. The aim of this will be to better crawl mobile specific architecture that makes heavy use of languages such as Java and JavaScript, as well as defining clearly if the site is mobile friendly or not.

How does this affect the SERPs?

Well, Google will show a completely different mobile-only search results page for users on mobile devices. This essentially means two different Googles, one for mobile users and one for everybody else.

The aim of this is to deliver a more mobile-friendly search result. If you search using desktop, Google you will no longer receive results linking to mobile apps for example, while the new mobile friendly search results will be more in tune with on the move searching, such as local searches based around your physical location.

What you need to do to get into Google's mobile search results

You probably already guessed, but having a mobile friendly website is the key here.

If your website is currently not a responsive design, that resizes and simplifies when necessary depending on the device and resolution, then you should be looking at investing in this right now.

On top of that, the site needs to be fast loading. This means making sure images are optimised, scripts and inline code are minimised or eradicated and making use of a Content Delivery Network (CDN see: http://en.wikipedia.org/wiki/Content_delivery _network) where possible.

Another thing the update will be looking for is simplified navigation (the menu system for your website). Google Webmaster Tools highlights webpages that it has crawled and has decided are not simplified enough, in navigation terms, for mobile users, so make sure you sign up for a Webmaster Tools account (see Chapter 6 for more information about this tool).

More complex menus, or small menus, that would be difficult for a mobile user to click on using their fingers or thumbs are now being highlighted in your Webmaster tools account.

I would suggest that in terms of your future strategy you should be looking at a single website that is simplified and responsive across all device types. It is far more expensive to try and develop parallel desktop and mobile friendly websites, so this Google update should be seen as an incentive to unify your future development.

How can I check if my website is being affected by Google's Mobile-Friendly Update?

There is a tool (available here: https://www.google.co.uk/webmasters/tools/mobile-friendly/) that you can use to check all the pages of your website for mobile friendliness.

Simply enter the URL and it will either tell you the page is mobile friendly, or it will return a list of the things you need to do to achieve that.

From that you can create a development plan to address the issues right across your website in a cost-effective manner, or you have something to send to your web developer to fix.

It's not time to worry about your core search engine rankings…..yet!

Google's Zineb Ait Bahajji, from the Webmaster Trends team, was quoted as saying at SMX Munich 2015 that the mobile friendly update would have more of an impact on the search results than the Penguin or Panda updates.

This was at the heart of the panic. But what he was referring to was mobile search results, not all search results. So it's vital to understand that the mobile friendly update only affects the existing mobile search results.

If your website has ten pages and five pass the criteria for being mobile friendly, then they will potentially benefit while the others do not. This is a vital point – it is going to be done on a page-by-page basis and, importantly, in real time.

So it won't be like the Penguin algorithm update, where a penalty lasted until the next update - which was over 12 months in one case!

Change the page structure, submit it for indexing and benefit when it passes the mobile friendly criteria.

But the takeaway is not to be complacent and definitely not to sit back and await developments.

A full mobile friendly algorithm is coming and it will be delivered to mobile device users. This means at some stage there will be a complete separation of Google's search results.

People are familiar with responsive design and enjoy the simpler navigation it brings. Don't see it as dumbing down of your online presence, see it as addressing the modern Internet user's needs and get on-board now.

Guest Blogging
In yet another "sky is falling" moment in the world of Google algorithm updates, it was proclaimed in 2014 that guest blogging was going to start being a sure-fire way to earn your site some negative ranking love.

Attacking guest blogging is one example of how the internet has changed since the release of Google's Penguin and Panda updates. When put together, Google's algorithm updates have worked on improving the quality of site content listed in search results.

One key aspect of this has been the Penguin updates. Google Penguin is about addressing the quality and relevance of links to web pages. Its aim has been to stamp out 'blackhat' tactics where link volume and anchor text from poor quality links have unduly influenced web page ranking.

How does guest blogging upset Google?

Google's Webmaster guidelines state a variety of reasons why your website might receive a manual or algorithmic penalty. One of these, relating to link building, states:

"Large-scale article marketing or guest posting campaigns with keyword rich anchor text links…"

Anchor text links refer to the words that are hyperlinked (clickable) to your website.

In terms of guest blogging, the problem is around generating articles that contain links to your own website, usually keyword links within the article, purely for that link.

This is one reason why article directories got hit in one of the rounds of algorithm updates. Poor quality content generated purely to build links, on what were basically content farms were devalued.

As soon as the easy win of submitting content to an article directory was removed, people began looking at guest blogging as a way of replacing that link building tactic. This in turn led to where we are now, where guest blogging is a target for Google.

Real guest blogging can still be a great tactic both in terms of building links and building traffic, but only if you understand what guest blogging should be and how to implement it properly.

What is guest blogging?

For as long as the Internet has existed, people have written articles for publication on third-party websites. In return for writing the article it is almost universal practice to credit the author with a link to their own site, usually in the form of a biography at the end of the article.

Guest blogging in its most noble form is no different to the freelance columnist in your newspaper, offering an independent opinion in writing.

Google even encouraged this in a way through its authorship program, which allowed web pages to individually be linked to a Google+ profile.

As soon as Google caught onto guest blogging manipulation, authorship was removed. But the horse had already bolted, and if they hold their hands up, it was partly Google's fault for encouraging people to use Authorship.

How do I know if it is worth me taking the risk?

In the post-Penguin world many people have turned away from guest blogging. To quote Matt Cutts, head of web spam at Google, many people have taken the advice he stated at the time:

"So stick a fork in it: guest blogging is done…"

But despite that, many people do still write guest blog posts and it works well for them. They are also not receiving penalties because of the way they are going about it. So to successfully guest blog you need to understand how to be seen as doing it for the right reasons.

A good link to your site is one that comes from a high quality and relevant website. It will also be an active site with a history, strong audience and social media buzz. All the signals will tell Google that the site is not there to generate links.

In essence, guest blogging is worth it if you change your mindset on why you are guest blogging. Gaining a link should be a secondary concern. What is positive about guest blogging is it allows you to broaden your audience, demonstrate expertise and highlight your brand.

Tips for successful guest blogging

If you want to convince Google that you are guest blogging for the right reasons then the best thing to do is make sure you are following a simple set of guidelines to demonstrate that.

1. Only submit high quality content

Your article should be completely original, impeccably constructed and should offer a personal and unique viewpoint. Simply by reading it, somebody should be able to tell that this is a valuable piece of content.

2. Be careful about including links

If you are referencing other web pages from within your article, make sure these are reputable and relevant. If you are intending to link to your own website within your article then make it a highly relevant link and ensure you also link to other high quality resources within your niche. This will make it less likely that Google will decide your link is purely an attempt to build links.

3. Encourage social interaction

Google will be looking for social connections to help spot if your article is being liked by human beings.

So encourage discussion at the end of your article, share it with your own social media following and encourage them to read it and share it.

4. Only guest blog on reputable sites

Unless a site is well established and has a strong following then I would suggest you do not submit the guest blog post to it. It's also advisable to have some sort of personal interaction with the person who runs a site to ensure that integrity.

Make a guest blogging decision based on what is best for your brand

You may decide that there are other ways to build links. Guest blogging is under the microscope so if you are to use it as a method of link building then it is not something that should be seen as a five-minute job.

However, if you invest serious time and effort into producing great guest blog posts and getting them published on high quality sites then guest blogging is still a great strategy for producing links, traffic, social media exposure and building of your brand.

Directory Links

Whilst link building is seen as an outdated practice, Google still acknowledges links to your website as a sign that your website is worth linking to. Having high quality links from relevant websites to your site will benefit your search engine rankings. It's how you go about obtaining these links that's important to ensure the longevity of your search engine positions.

Links from directories were abused by people trying to game the system and build a large quantity of links to their websites in a short space of time.

Sadly, this technique worked, but with Google getting smarter, these types of low quality links from directories are something to avoid.

There are, however, legitimate directories you may want to list your website under. For example, Yell.com and Thomson Local (in the UK) are well established business directories which are seen as trustworthy by Google. They should also send traffic to your website and this traffic should be people actively searching for your products and services.

This is key to building links - any link you acquire should have the potential to send qualified traffic to your website. If you're acquiring links for the sake of improving your search engine position, you could be jeopardising the future of your website when Google catches up with you.

If you're looking to build a few links to your site, look for directories that are relevant to your business such as trading bodies, institutions and organisations that represent your industry. Avoid any directory that mentions SEO, link building, free links etc. These are directories set up to allow people to build low quality links and if they haven't already been penalised by Google, it's only a matter of time before they are.

Local SEO and Citations
If you're a local business, a shop, restaurant or therapist where customers visit you at your premises and are likely to search for your service in a specific geographical area, you need to make sure your business can be found.

Google is able to recognise when your business is being talked about or listed on a website whether there's a link to your website or not. These mentions are known as *citations*.

Citations provide Google with information about your business such as its name, physical address, and phone number. Google will use this information to present the most relevant results to someone searching for your products or services in your locality.

You need to bear this in mind if your business details change as Google could get confused about where you're based or your contact details.

In this chapter, I have looked at a few 'off-page' ways of improving your overall search engine rankings and discussed some of the pitfalls if you get it wrong. You need to keep in mind your motive at all times and put the user before Google. If you don't, you are at risk of receiving a penalty yourself.

In the next chapter, I'll go into more detail about how to avoid such a penalty and what to do if you suspect you have been hit by one.

5. How can I avoid a Google penalty?

Few things are more devastating to a business which depends on search engine traffic to generate sales than getting whacked over the head with a Google penalty. Literally overnight the heart of any company can be ripped out.

If you do your own search engine optimisation work then it's obviously vital that you understand what could cause Google to give you a penalty, which is basically a negative ranking modifier applied within their search engine algorithm. The result is your website is moved down a few pages in the search results, or it's removed completely.

But just as importantly, how do you know if somebody you have employed to carry out this work is doing damage to your online reputation that you may never recover from?

So it's very important that you understand how you can avoid a Google penalty in order to protect your business, which means being aware of the key things that can generate one.

What is a Google penalty anyway?

Google has become the world's top search engine because it has worked hard to ensure that people receive high quality and relevant results when they search. This has allowed them to generate huge revenues from advertising.

To protect their market position Google works hard on its algorithm. This algorithm contains more than 200 ranking factors, which, when put together, determine the best sites to display for any search term entered.

To try and stop people from manipulating the system, Google has developed a set of rules for website owners around what is expected of them. These include detailed quality guidelines that are pretty unambiguous.

If you break the rules then you could be hit by a penalty. Google penalties come in two forms, automatic algorithmic penalties and manual penalties (manual actions).

Let's look at the types of penalty you can get

Manual penalties are dished out by the search quality team. Sites are reported or flagged and then receive a human visit.
If the guidelines are compromised then the site is manually penalised.

The automatic penalties come in two main forms:

Penguin.
The Penguin updates are refinements to the Google algorithm which specifically look for low quality links that point to a website. As well as the quality of links, they also analyse link anchor text. If the only links pointing at your site are stuffed full of keywords for example, then that's not looking natural and you can expect to be sniffed out eventually.

Natural link anchor text should include things like "click here", "visit website", "www.yourdomain.com" as well as your keywords.

Panda.

The Panda updates are all about looking at the quality of what is on each web page. If your site contains duplicate content, thin content (for example, a sales page with just a few paragraphs (of keyword-stuffed text) on it, or just generally low quality content such as machine generated content (usually known as spun content), then you could be the target of a Panda update.

How will I know if I've been hit by a Google penalty?

If you keep on top of your website's metrics around rankings and visitors then there are several clear-cut signs to watch out for. Not all of these are immediate signs that your site has been hit by a penalty, but if those signs persist then it's time for alarm bells to start ringing.

You should always have your website hooked up with Google's Webmaster Tools. This is free for anyone with a Google account, so the first step is to get your website set-up inside Google Webmaster Tools.

One of the first places you can be made aware of a penalty is within your Webmaster Tools account. You will usually receive a notification telling you that unnatural linking has been found, or that you have been penalised.

The second thing you can do quickly is to search for your site by brand or company name. Unless it is something really common, then it should appear on the first page. If you search for it and you can't find it anywhere then that is a real red light.

Another big clue is if your traffic suddenly decreases sharply.
If you have been removed from the index then it will almost completely disappear overnight, if you have been hit with a smaller penalty then you should see a dip where the rankings are taking a hit. Use your Google Analytics reports to detect a drop in search engine traffic. There's more information about Google Analytics and Google Webmaster Tools in chapter 6.

Tips to avoid getting a Google penalty

Okay, so now we understand exactly what a Google penalty is and what it looks like when you get one, let's discuss how you can avoid the entire situation in the first place.

The first thing you should do is to be completely familiar with Google's quality guidelines. If you're going to employ an outside agency to optimise your website then it's still vital you know about them, so that you can question the people who are going to be entrusted with your rankings (and potentially the future of your business).

Broadly, the ways to avoid a penalty are simply to stay within the boundaries of the quality guidelines:

Don't build shady links
Try to get natural links, but if you are building links make sure they are from trusted sources wherever possible. Also, make sure the anchor text of your links varies. Real people do not write online content with keyword links all over the place.

Create pages for people not search engines
Look at each page on your website and ask yourself if it adds value to a visitor's experience. In terms of future content, make sure you have a fully developed content marketing strategy in place so that your website develops into a strong resource that is obviously not set out to rank purely to push people through to sales content.

Make sure your site structure ticks all the boxes
This means making it a responsive design. It means having 'about', 'privacy', 'terms' and 'contact' pages. It means showing you are active on social media through displaying links to your accounts. It also means having a sitemap, a robots.txt file and nofollowed links where appropriate.

A **sitemap** is an XML file which lists all the pages on your website, with useful information for Google like how often they are updated and which you consider to be more important. This file can be generated using a sitemap generator (search Google for lots of free tools) and should be uploaded to the root directory of your website (http://www.yourdomain.com/sitemap.xml)

A **robots.txt** file is used to control what Google crawls on your website. If you have areas of your website that you don't wish Google to add to its index, you can 'disallow' Googlebot from visiting these pages. As with a sitemap file, there are free tools out there to generate a robots.txt file and this should be uploaded to the root directory of your website (http://www.yourdomain.com/robots.txt)

Nofollowed links are links from one web page to another that you don't want Google to follow. You might do this if the site you're linking to isn't of a high quality and you don't want the association with it. You may also add a nofollow attribute to a link within a paid advert as Google frowns upon people paying for links to their site and recommends you ask the website owner to add a nofollow attribute to the link.

My final word here is around being calm and consistent.

If revenues are down, or your rankings are not improving then it can be too easy to get desperate or cut corners.

Suddenly it seems a great idea to throw money at somebody to create 1000 relevant links to your website, or undertake some other type of "Blackhat" strategy.

Just don't do it.

Stick to your guns by reviewing your content and building a proper content marketing strategy for the future. Look at how you can engage through social media to drive traffic to your website, encourage sharing and encourage natural link building.

Submit your site to places that are appropriate in order to build links and traffic. Build off-site content, such as guest blog posting, to build links and traffic. But do it in a structured and relevant manner.

Getting a Google penalty is just the final stage in a journey that started with somebody making poor decisions, so make sure that your business makes good ones.

What to do if you suspect you've been hit by a Google penalty

First of all, don't panic!

You should check Google Webmaster Tools - if you don't have an account, it's worth setting one up as it's completely free. In here, Google will let you know if it has spotted something amiss with your site.

Quite often it's because Google has found links pointing to your site which look shady, manipulative or against their guidelines. What you need to do in this situation is to identify those links (Google should show you which ones it doesn't like) and do your best to remove them. This can be done by contacting the webmaster of the website linking to you and asking them to take down the link.

If the website is shady, you'll probably find that there is no one managing the site or no way of getting in touch with them. If this is the case, you can use Google's 'Disavow' tool within the Webmaster Tools suite. The Disavow tool lets you tell Google which links to ignore. It does not guarantee that Google will pay attention to this, but it's a step in the right direction and shows Google you're serious about cleaning up your act.

Once you have done this you can submit a reconsideration request to Google through Webmaster Tools to ask Google to review the changes you have made and consider reinstating you in the search results.

If there's no warnings in Webmaster Tools, it could be that you've fallen victim to a Google algorithm update. The actions you need to take to recover from this kind of penalty depend on the update that affected your website.

First of all, open your Google Analytics reports (another free tool if you're not already using it) and filter traffic down so you're looking at just traffic from organic search (unpaid). You should see a drop in traffic on the graph at the time the algorithm update hit.

The next step is to then see which update was rolled out on that day. You can use tools such as Moz's Google Algorithm Change History document here: https://moz.com/google-algorithm-change

This will tell you what the update was and what kind of websites or practices triggered the update. Then you should have enough information to be able to rectify what was wrong with your site and submit a reconsideration request.

Penalties sound scary and, if you rely on Google solely for your website traffic, it can be disastrous for a business to disappear from the search results even if it's just for a few days. The best way to avoid penalties altogether is to stick to Google's guidelines when it comes to optimising your site. If you pay someone to optimise your site for you, make sure they are not putting you at risk of a penalty by requesting to see the work they have done.

If you are doing your own SEO, read on for some useful tools to help you along the way.

6. What tools are there to help me optimise my website?

I've mentioned a few tools already in previous chapters, but it's worth highlighting some key tools here that will help you monitor your website and make sure your website is optimised.

There are absolutely hundreds of tools out there and it wouldn't be helpful to list all of them here, so I have just picked out a few tools that I use on a regular basis and form the foundation for most SEO audits, campaigns and monthly reports that I do for clients.

Google's Keyword Planner
This is a great place to start any SEO campaign as it will give you focus for optimising your pages.

The tool is part of Google AdWords and is free to use:
https://adwords.google.co.uk/KeywordPlanner

Once you're in your Google AdWords account, the Keyword Planner can be found under Tools on the top menu.

The information that this can give you is invaluable and will save you a lot of hours. You will find reports that shoe you which search terms are used to find your products and services and how many people are typing these into Google each month.

It will also show you the competition for each keyword, what traffic you should expect and how much you would be paying if you choose to advertise on Google.

It may be that you think you know the keywords that people use to find your website, but assumptions can be dangerous and Google will show you exactly what people search for and also give you other keyword ideas that you may not have thought of.

These keywords with high volumes of people searching for them will drive the most traffic, so it's these keywords that you want to be including on your website.

If you are in a particularly competitive industry and you notice your main keywords are all coming up as 'high' for competition, you might want to investigate optimising for more niche terms or what is known in SEO as 'long tail' search terms.

These are typically 3+ words long and are much more specific. The benefit of optimising for long tail search queries is that the searchers often know exactly what they are looking for and if your website provides this, they are more likely to buy.

Google Trends
Another free tool from Google, Trends shows you the popularity of certain keywords and phrases over the last 10 years: http://google.co.uk/trends

This is useful to see how terminology changes and goes in and out of fashion over time. For example, if you type 'solar panels' into Google Trends you'll see how the term increased in popularity from 2004 to 2008 where it then reached a plateau and, if anything, has now started to decline slightly.

Trends will let you see search popularity by country - really useful if you export goods and services into other markets to make sure you're using the right terminology for your target market. A good example is the term 'caravan' in the UK refers to a type of leisure vehicle towed behind a car, whereas in the US, if you search for 'caravan' you're likely to find references to the Dodge Caravan car or the verb 'to caravan' as they refer to the leisure vehicle as a 'trailer'.

You can also use the Forecast feature to get Google's insight into whether the term will continue in popularity over the next couple of years as well as comparing search terms side by side to see which is the more popular.

SEO Site Checkup
This is a third party tool which lets you run a limited number of reports for free before asking you to register. You can choose the reports you want, but basically it will produce a 20+ page document highlighting just about every important aspect of SEO and whether your website meets its guidelines.

Visit http://seositecheckup.com/ to run your report. You'll see it also looks at social signals (whether your website is being talked about on social media) and whether your website is mobile friendly.

There is some jargon in these reports and a lot of techie stuff and although the explanations are good for professional SEOs, you may find that some of the wording isn't particularly user friendly.

Open Site Explorer

This tool comes with limited functionality on the free version and the paid for version starts at $99 per month with Moz membership, so you need to be serious about using this tool if you are going to be paying for it each month. That said, there is a free 30 day trial which is simple to cancel, so it's worth trying it out for free to see what it does.

Open Site Explorer shows you the links pointing to your website from other websites. It will tell you how many websites link to yours (linking root domains), and how many links you have in total - some sites may link more than once so the number of links should always be higher than the linking root domains.

It also gives you lots of useful information about the links pointing to your site in terms of the quality of links and how well Google trusts the linking site. This is shown as Domain Authority and Page Authority which work on a scale from 1 - 100 where 100 is excellent and 0 is not so great.

You will also see whether the link to your site is a text link and if so, what the linking text (anchor text) reads, or whether it's an image that is linked to your website - quite often this is your logo or a button they says 'Visit Site'.

You can separate out internal and external links too. Internal links are those which go from one page of your website to another. External links are those that come from a completely different website to yours.

This tool is essential for competitor analysis too. Not only can you check the links to your own website, but you can check the links to your competitors' too. Where are they getting links from? Is there an opportunity to get a few links from these sources too? Obviously, you need to make sure that these links are genuine and not low quality.

Look for links from blogs where the blog owner may write about you too or allow you to write a guest post for their blog.

Also look for trade bodies and organisations that link to your competitors. Chances are they have a business directory that you could be a part of too.

Google Webmaster Tools
I've mentioned this one before, but as another free tool from Google, you'd be crazy not to check it out and set up an account if you manage your own website.

It will alert you to any issues with the content of your site including duplicate page titles and meta descriptions. It will also show you links to your website and the keywords Google associates with your site.

You'll also see any errors that Google has discovered like pages that show an error like 404 'not found' errors.

For webmasters it's an essential tool, but it's pretty useful for optimising your website too, so visit https://www.google.com/webmasters/tools/ and set up your website.

This may require a little help from a web developer, but it isn't a big task, so don't be paying someone hundreds to set this up.

Google Analytics
If you don't have Google Analytics (or another web analytics software package) installed on your website, do it now!

Analytics will show you how well your SEO efforts are paying off. You can see traffic from search engines over time and how long people stay on your site, the pages they view and whether they buy anything or submit an enquiry.

You can even see what devices people use to access your website which gives you a good indication as to whether you need to make your site mobile-friendly.

This information is going to tell you the value of traffic from Google and other search engines as well as social media sites. It's also going to show you progress over time and give you the evidence to assess what activities are sending the most traffic to your website.

These are just a few of the core tools any website owner should be utilising as a basis for optimising and monitoring their website. If you're paying someone to optimise your site for you, these tools will come in handy to run your own reports and assess the work they are doing.

Conclusion

SEO is probably one of the more technical areas of Digital Marketing so if you've read this far and still feel you need a little more hand holding, I can recommend Moz's Beginner's Guide to SEO, available to read and download here: https://moz.com/beginners-guide-to-seo

You don't need to know everything there is to know about SEO in order to see your website rank well in Google's search results. The key things to remember are:

1. Make sure you are optimising your website for the right keywords - use Google's Keyword Planner to see how many people are searching for your chosen keywords.
2. Place your keywords on your website within your page titles, meta descriptions, text and image alt attributes.
3. Be active on social media, share your content and aim to drive as much relevant traffic to your website as possible.

4. Never do anything to your website that you wouldn't do if search engines didn't exist - stick to the guidelines that Google gives us to ensure you don't fall victim to a Google penalty in the future. https://support.google.com/webmasters/answer/35769?hl=en

If you choose to hire someone to manage your SEO for you, you should feel more confident in being able to communicate with them and understand where your money is being spent.

If you feel empowered to optimise your own website, excellent! I wish you the best of luck!

Heather

For more resources and books to help you promote your small business online, visit: http://skittish.academy/books